What Is Solid?

by Caroline Hutchinson

Look at this house. It is made of stones. Stones are solid.

3

Here is a car. It is made
of metal. Metal is solid, too.

This is a vase. It is made
of glass. Glass is solid.

Look at the bridge. The bridge is made of metal. Do you think it is solid?

Here is a glass of juice. The glass is solid. The juice is not.

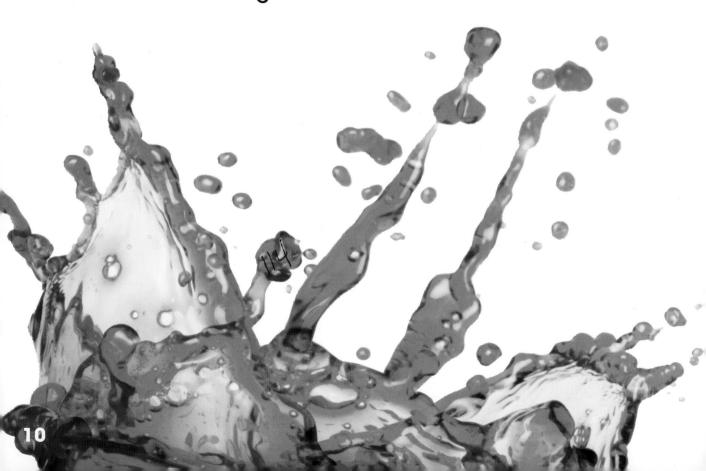

Look at the rain on the window. The window is solid. Do you think the rain is solid, too?

Here is an orange. It is solid.

Do you think the orange juice
is solid?

What do you think is solid?

What do you think is not?